Your Living Years

Discovering Through Questions

By

TERRYMILAMGEASLIN

Dedication

To Paul, my husband, thank you for being my partner, my confidant, and my love. Since I began this journey over two decades ago, you have encouraged me every step of the way.

To Robin, my daughter, thank you for being there with me throughout the process of composing this book. You have kept me centered and nudging me to expand this to the quality that it truly has become. I honor the profound impact you have had and the invaluable role you have played in shaping this book.

To Shane, my son, I am filled with gratitude for the honor of being your mother. Your kindness, strength, and inherent goodness illuminate the world around you, touching the lives of all who have the privilege of knowing you.

To Brooke, my daughter-in-law, taking care of your family is a special responsibility and privilege and I thank you for that. Your presence in my life is a gift that I cherish deeply.

To River, my granddaughter, you are a shining star in my life, bringing boundless joy, laughter, and love into every moment we share. From the sparkle in your eyes to the warmth of your hugs, you fill my world with endless wonder and delight.

To Malcolm, my grandson, as I watch you grow and explore the world around you, I am filled with wonder at the unlimited potential that exists within each of you. Your kindness, creativity, and resilience inspire me to see the world through fresh eyes and embrace each day with a sense of awe and possibility.

My family, past, and present, is the most important part of my life. Cherishing the memories of those who came before me while treasuring the moments shared with those in the present has brought me a profound sense of fulfillment and purpose.

Foreword

In Your Living Years: Discovering Through Questions, Terry Geaslin invites you on a journey—one that transcends time and connects you with the very essence of your existence. Through the art of storytelling and the power of simple questions, this book opens the door to a world of discovery, where the treasures of your family's past await.

In today's fast-paced world, where technology often replaces heartfelt conversation, Terry reminds us of the profound value of our personal narratives. With a gentle hand and an unwavering passion for preserving heritage, she guides us through the process of uncovering the untold stories that lie within our own living years.

From the laughter of childhood memories to the wisdom of generations past, each question in this book serves as a beacon, illuminating the path to our shared history. Whether you are a seasoned personal historian or a curious family member, Terry has crafted a collection of questions that speak to the soul, igniting a spark of curiosity and wonder in us all.

As you embark on this journey of discovery, may you find solace in the stories of your ancestors, strength in the resilience of their journeys, and inspiration in the legacy they've left behind. And may Your Living Years be more than just a book—it is a tribute to the timeless art of storytelling, a celebration of the human experience, and a testament to the enduring power of family.

So, dear reader, I invite you to turn the page, to delve into the depths of your own living years, and to uncover the stories that have shaped your life. For within these pages lies the key to unlocking the mysteries of your past and embracing the beauty of your present.

With warm regards,

Robin Geaslin

Contents

Introduction

Are you at that age yet when you wonder about, "Who am I? What do I know about my family's history?" Of course, the primary sources to go to are your parents, your grandparents, or if you are fortunate, your great-grandparents. Typically, people gather basic information like names, dates, and places, but what about those stories that you may have heard from time to time through the years? Were they written down, or did they just fade away through time? You had a best friend in high school, but what about your mother's closest friend in school? What were high school days like for her? What was her favorite aunt's personality? What was her family's first automobile?

Years ago, I embarked on a business venture of documenting family histories. Conducting comprehensive research, I consulted the Chamber of Commerce for guidance, sought legal advice, and meticulously formulated numerous questions. Despite all my measures, participations at seminars and marketing events, the reception was lukewarm. People seemed disinterested when I mentioned personal histories for their families. Their reactions often suggested either an assumption that their children were already well-informed, or they simply had a lack of interest. Preserving your family's history ensures that their legacy endures across generations. Initiating this endeavor for posterity is crucial, and the time to embark is now. As life progresses and priorities shift, we come to understand the fleeting nature of our time with loved ones, underscoring the importance of capturing and safeguarding our ancestral heritage. Begin with a parent, a sibling, or even yourself.

I long for a book authored by my grandmothers, detailing their lives, which I could have later passed down to my children and grandchildren. Through its pages, we would have had a peek into our ancestors' lives as it happened generations ago. This is not about bestsellers, but rather the invaluable chronicle of your own family history. What a truly priceless gift.

Recording personal histories extends beyond family circles. Genealogists, writers, educational institutions, nonprofit organizations, therapists, executives, and entrepreneurs can all benefit from documenting life stories. To ease this process, utilize various tools such as pen and paper, digital recorders, smartphones, audio editing software, cameras, scanners, and transcription services.

Embrace the journey, even if it means not capturing every detail. Your efforts will be appreciated by your family now and in the future. While some questions may seem trivial, they prompt valuable discussions and evoke cherished memories. Remember, lost lives equate to lost histories, so make the endeavor enjoyable and meaningful.

Your Name

What is the origin or meaning behind your first name?

Were you named after someone who was important to your parents?

Do you have any nicknames associated with your name?

If so, how did you acquire them?

Do you feel your name reflects your personality or identity?

Have you ever considered changing your name?

If so, why and did you?

Are there any stories about your name that you find interesting or amusing?

How do you feel about the spelling or pronunciation of your name?

Has it ever caused any issues?

Do you know the history behind your last name?

Have you ever met someone with the same full name as yours?

How did you feel about it?

Your Mother /Grandmothers

(I have used "her" and "you" interchangeably. Start with your grandmother, if possible, then your mother, then hopefully yourself.)

What is/was the name of your mother/grandmother?

Any special reason for that name?

Are there any stories about her name?

What was her given name?

When and where was she born?

Where did she grow up?

If she immigrated here, do you know when that happened?

What were the circumstances for the move?

Did other family members come with her?

Are there still family members back in the home country?

Did she ever return for visits?

Did any family members come here to visit?

Does she have any siblings?

What are/were their names and age differences?

Was she closer to one more than the other(s)?

Do you have any great-aunts or great-uncles that you have memories of?

Was any of them more special than the other(s)?

What is your earliest memory of your mother/grandmother?

Can you describe a typical day with her during your childhood?

What are some of the lessons or values you learned from her?

Do you have any special traditions with her?

What is one thing you admire most about her?

Can you share a memorable story involving her?

What was your funniest memory?

What was your saddest memory?

What are some of her hobbies or interests?

How do you celebrate Mother's Day or family birthdays?

What is the best advice she has ever given you?

How do you keep in touch with her if you live far apart, and how often?

What is one thing you wish you could tell her if you had the chance?

How has her influence shaped who you are today?

Describe your mother's/grandmother's looks.

Do others say you look like her?

Do you feel that you look like her?

What were your mother's/grandmother's best/worst qualities?

Are you like her in any way?

What was your relationship like with your mother?

How has your relationship with her evolved over time?

Did you get along with your mother/grandmother?

If not, did you ever make amends?

Did your mother/grandmother have any free time?

What did she do?

Did she have any birthmarks or scars?

How did she get it/them?

Did she cook?

What were your favorite meals that she would cook for you?

Do you have any favorite recipes passed down from your mother/grandmother?

How about appliances?

Did she have to use a washboard to scrub the clothes, or a wringer type washer?

What about the refrigerator?

Did they have block ice to cool the food?

And defrosting those things. Was that a chore?

Did your parents entertain at home often?

What did you enjoy the most about entertaining?

Did she work outside the home?

What type of work did she do?

What type of house did she live in as a child and as a grown-up?

What was home life like?

School life. Describe the school(s) she attended.

What were the teaching methods back then?

If someone was disciplined, what methods were used?

Were extracurricular activities at her school, and if so, was she involved in any?

How were the grades divided?

Did she graduate?

Did she have other children besides you?

Had she previously been married?

Can she elaborate on that?

Did she talk to you about her wedding day/dress?

Where did she go on her honeymoon?

When and where did your parents meet?

When and where did they get married?

How old were they when they got married?

When did she die?

What were the circumstances of her death?

Where is she buried?

Growing up, what was your family's religion?

Do you still practice it today?

If not, can you elaborate?

Do you have any special memories you want to share?

If you could thank your mother for one thing, what would it be?

Your Father /Grandfathers

(I have used "him" and "you" interchangeably. Start with your grandfather, if possible, then your father, then hopefully yourself.)

What is/was the name of your father/grandfather?

Any special reason for that name?

Are there any stories about his name?

When and where was he born?

Where did he grow up?

If he immigrated here, do you know when that happened?

What were the circumstances for the move?

Did other family members come with him?

Are there any family members still back in their home country?

Did he ever return for visits?

Does he have any siblings?

What are/were their names?

Was he closer to one more than the others?

What is your earliest memory of him?

Can you describe a typical day spent with him during your childhood?

What are some of the lessons or values you learned from him?

Do you have any special traditions with him?

What is one thing you admire most about him?

Can you share a memorable story with him?

What are some of his favorite hobbies or interests?

How do you celebrate Father's Day or birthdays?

What is the best advice he has ever given you?

Do you have any favorite activities you enjoy doing with him?

How do you stay in touch with him if you live far apart, and how often?

What is one thing you wish you could tell him if you had the chance?

How has his influence shaped who you are today?

What did his father look like?

Do others say you look like him?

Do you feel you look like him?

How has your relationship with him evolved over time?

What were his father's best/worst qualities?

Are you like him in any way?

Did you get along with your father? If not, did you ever make amends?

School life. Describe the school(s) he attended.

What were the teaching methods back then?

If someone was disciplined back then, what methods were used?

Were extracurricular activities at his school, and if so, was he involved in any?

How were the grades divided?

Did he graduate?

What type of work did he do?

If they owned a farm, have them explain about it.

Was it a ranch or a farm?

How many acres did they have?

What type of animals did they raise?

What type of house did he live in as a child and as a grown-up?

What was home life like?

Did he have other children besides you?

Had he previously been married?

Can he elaborate on that?

When did he die?

What were the circumstances of his death?

Where is he buried?

Do you have any special memories you want to share?

If you could thank your father for one thing, what would it be?

Your Aunts/Uncles and Other Family Matters

What is your fondest memory with your aunt/uncle?

Can you describe a special tradition you share with your aunt/uncle?

How would you describe your relationship with your aunt/uncle?

What qualities do you admire most about them?

Do you have any memorable stories about your aunt/uncle?

How has your aunt/uncle influenced your life?

Are there any valuable lessons you have learned from your aunt/uncle?

What are some of your favorite activities to do together with your aunt/uncle?

How do you typically celebrate holidays or special occasions with your aunt/uncle?

Have you ever gone on any memorable trips with your aunt/uncle?

What is one thing you appreciate most about your aunt/uncle?

How do you stay connected with your aunt/uncle if you live far apart, and how often?

Do you have any favorite foods or recipes that remind you of your aunt/uncle?

If you could thank your aunt/uncle for one thing, what would it be?

Are/were there any "black sheep" in the family?

Was either of your parents the "black sheep?"

Can they elaborate if they were?

Were there any family heirlooms/property, etc., that have been handed down from generation to generation?

What are they, and how old are they?

Where are they now?

Are there any stories about famous or infamous relatives on either side of the family?

Brothers and Sisters

Do you have any siblings?

What are/were their names?

Where were they born?

If they are deceased, how, when, and where are they buried?

What is your position in the family?

Youngest, oldest?

What were the advantages or disadvantages?

What is your earliest memory of your brother/sister?

Can you describe a typical day spent with your brother/sister during your childhood?

What are some of the shared interests or hobbies you have with your brother/sister?

How would you describe your relationship with your brother/sister?

How has it changed over the years?

What qualities do you admire most in your brother/sister?

Can you share a memorable story involving your brother/sister?

Do you have any special traditions that you share with your brother/sister?

How do you support each other during challenging times?

Have you ever experienced any sibling rivalry?

How did you resolve it?

What is one thing you appreciate most about having a brother/sister?

Are there any valuable lessons you have learned from your brother/sister?

How do you stay connected with your brother/sister if you live far apart and how often?

What are your hopes for the future of your relationship with your brother/sister?

Were you especially close to any of them?

Why do you feel that way?

What are some examples?

Did you wish you had more brothers and/or sisters?

Why?

Talk about your parent's philosophy about raising kids. Their discipline, rules, etc.

Are there any physical characteristics that run in your family?

Your Childhood-You and Your Family

When and where were you born?

Did your parents or family have stories about your birth?

Which parent did you favor the most?

Think back. What were your earliest memories?

How old were you?

Can you describe your favorite childhood toy or game?

What was your favorite book or movie as a child?

Can you share a memorable birthday party or celebration from your childhood?

Did you have chores when you were young, and what were they?

How did you feel about doing them?

What were the ramifications if you didn't?

Any good stories about that?

What did you do when you were a child that got you in the most trouble, and how did your parents handle it?

Can you describe a challenging or difficult moment from your childhood and how you overcame it?

Who cooked the meals?

Describe a typical family weekday meal.

Did you sit at the table every night, or did you sit around the TV while you ate?

Sunday dinner, was there anything special about that meal?

What was your favorite mealtime?

Why?

What did you like to eat?

What was your favorite food?

What kind of kitchen stove did your parents cook on?

Who did the ironing?

Did your mother buy or make your own clothes?

Did you learn how to cook?

Who taught you?

Did you learn how to sew?

What was the first thing you made?

How about crocheting, knitting, embroidering, painting, etc.?

Who taught you, and can you remember what was the first thing you made?

Did you ever learn the mechanics of a car?

If so, who taught you?

Did you take machine shop or woodworking in school?

Who taught you?

What were some of the things you made?

Did your family read or tell stories together?

Did you play any instruments, and did your family sing together?

What instrument did you play, and how old were you when you started?

Did you have any family pets? Tell me about them.

How did the family spend their evenings?

What about Sundays?

How did you get your mail?

Did your family keep in touch with distant family?

Were there any family reunions?

Did you visit relatives often?

Did your family have a good sense of humor, or were your parents more serious-minded?

Did you and/or your siblings play tricks on others?

Did you ever get caught?

What was the punishment?

How do you think your childhood experiences have influenced who you are today?

Where Did You Grow Up?

Did you live in the country or city?

What was it like to live there?

Describe the size of the town where you lived.

Where did your parents shop?

How large or small were the stores?

If you lived in a small town, or on a farm, did you ever go into the city to shop?

How often?

What was Main Street like?

What was the largest town/city you remember visiting when you were young?

What type of house did you live in as a child?

How many rooms did it have?

Were there other buildings on the same property?

If you moved during your childhood, tell me where and when.

What were the reasons for the move?

Relocating can evoke a range of emotions, including sadness and a hint of excitement or adventure. How did you feel about it?

Did you have a fireplace?

How was your home heated?

Did they have to buy fuel, or was it a chore, such as cutting firewood or hauling the coal?

Did you always have electricity? If not, when did you get it?

Did you ever use candles or kerosene lamps?

Did your house have a basement?

Did you have a favorite room besides your bedroom that you liked to play in?

Where did you store your food?

Where did you get your water?

Was it plentiful?

What methods were used to conserve water, if needed?

Did you have indoor plumbing or an outhouse?

How many seats did your outhouse have?

Do you have any fond or funny memories of the outhouse?

Where did you sleep?

Did you have your own room?

Who did you share it with?

Did you have your own bed?

Were there any home curses concerning the house you lived in?

Were there any notable people living in your hometown? Explain.

Were there any home cures or wives' tales for curing any ailments?

Did they work?

Tell about any of your neighbors.

Who were your friends in the neighborhood?

In the evening, what time did you get to stay outside before you were called home?

What were your favorite things to play with your friends inside or outside?

Any exceptional stories that you want to share?

Transportation

Did you ever travel on a train when you were young?

When was the first time you flew on a plane?

Did your family own a horse and buggy?

Did you have a bike? Describe it.

How old were you when you learned how to ride your bike?

What was the furthest from your house that you rode?

Did you ride your bike to school?

When did your family buy their first car?

What was the make and color?

How much did it cost then?

Where did your family go on vacation?

How did you travel?

What was your favorite vacation when you were young?

Did you ever get to take a friend on vacation?

Days, Seasons, and Special Occasions

What did Saturdays mean to you?

What did Sundays mean to you?

Describe the perfect:

Winter day

Spring day

Summer day

Fall day

What was your favorite season?

Did you attend church on Sundays or any other days of the week?

What role did religion play in your life?

Where did you attend church?

What was the name of the church?

Did you attend church regularly or take part in a ministry?

Did you go to a religious school?

Holidays can mean different things: time off work, gathering with friends and family, eating special treats, or just relaxing.

What did holidays mean to you as a child?

Tell me about Halloween. Did you go Trick or Treat, stay at home and hand out candy, or go to parties?

Do you have any memorable Halloweens?

Describe getting a Christmas tree as a child. When did you put it up, and how did you decorate it?

How did you spend Christmas or Hanukkah?

What food was served for these special occasions?

What kind of gifts did you receive?

Which gift stands out the most in all your Christmas'?

Did your family celebrate Easter?

Did you dress up for Easter?

What food was served for these special occasions?

How and where did you celebrate the Fourth of July?

Any special memories of that holiday?

Were there any other special occasions your family celebrated?

Can you elaborate?

How was your birthday celebrated?

What kinds of gifts did you receive on your birthday?

How did you keep cool during the summers?

What did you wear in the winter to keep warm?

Did you have to walk to school in the snow?

If it snowed where you lived, did they close schools when it snowed?

Did you ever go surfing?

Family Livelihood

What did your father do for a living?

Did he ever express how he felt about his job?

Did he encourage or discourage you from going into the same line of
work?

Did your mother ever work outside the home?

Did she feel she had to?

Did you or your siblings contribute to the family income?

When did you get your first job?

Where did you work?

What was your starting income?

Do you remember the first big purchase you made with your money?

Did your family have a garden?

Who did the work in the garden?

What kinds of vegetables did you grow?

Did your family have fruit trees?

What kind of fruit?

Did your family sell any of the produce?

Did anyone in the family do any canning?

Did your family raise cattle, sheep, goats, etc.?

Did you raise chickens?

Did you have cows for milking or meat on the table?

Did you make your own butter or cheese?

Was this your family's only income?

While you were growing up, did you have a sense of whether your family was rich or poor?

What would you say now about your family's economic circumstances when you were growing up?

How did your family's personal financial situation affect you?

Did it give or deprive you of special opportunities?

Elementary School

What year did you start school?

Do you have any good memories of that?

Where did you go to elementary school?

What did the school look like?

How many rooms did it have?

Do you remember the smell of the school?

What sticks out to you?

Now, I would like for you to think back to an incident in grade school that you remember well…what was going on?

What are some other memories of your elementary school years?

How did you go to school? Did you go alone or with others?

How far did you live from the school?

What time did you have to be at school?

Can you remember the names of your teachers?

Who was your favorite, and why?

What did you do during recess?

What did you typically eat at lunchtime?

What was your favorite subject?

What subject did you dread, and why?

How were your grades in grammar school?

What time did the school let out?

Did your school have fairs or carnivals, such as Halloween Carnivals?

Explain.

Friends and Games

How did you spend your summers during grade school?

What did you do for recreation?

Did your siblings have any hobbies?

Was there a hobby that you wished you could have done?

Who was your best friend?

What did you and your friends do when you got together?

Did you have a childhood hideout? Explain.

Detail a "sound" from your childhood.

What was it?

When did you hear it?

What memories or emotions did it evoke?

Did you and your playmates play any organized sports, dance, or gymnastics?

Did you have any childhood heroes?

Did you ever learn to swim?

If not, do you remember why?

Did you have a favorite swimming place?

Did you take part in youth organizations: 4H, Scouts, etc.?

How did your free time contribute to your personality?

Were you a sports fan?

What was your favorite sports/team?

Did you go camping?

Where was your favorite place to camp?

Did you have a favorite blanket or pillow that you had to take with you when you went on trips?

Did you have a favorite toy?

Do you remember your favorite colors and flowers?

Has that changed?

Middle /Intermediate /Junior High School Memories

What years did you attend middle school?

Where did you live during this time?

Describe the layout of the school.

Describe a typical day during your middle school days.

How many teachers did you have during the day?

What were the teaching methods?

Was discipline an important part of school?

What type of discipline were you aware of and did you ever experience any practices?

Did you take part in any sports, music, choir, campus organizations, etc.?

Now, I want you to think back to an incident in middle school that you remember well…what was going on?

How were your grades in middle school?

What subject did you enjoy?

Were there any classes you dreaded attending?

Did you have a favorite teacher? Explain.

What kinds of kids did you associate with?

Who were your best friends during middle school?

Are you still in contact with any of them?

If you could change one thing about your middle school years, what would it have been?

High School Memories

Where and what years did you go to high school?

Where did you live during this time?

Describe the layout of the school.

Describe a typical day during your high school days.

Now, I would like for you to think back to an incident in high school that you remember well…what was going on?

What were the teaching methods?

Was discipline an important part of school?

What type of discipline were you aware of and did you ever experience any practices?

How were your grades in high school?

Did you graduate, and in what year?

Did you walk across the stage, and how did you feel?

What subjects did you enjoy?

What class(es) did you dislike?

Did you have a favorite teacher?

What social groups did you belong to in high school?

Did you take part in any sports, music, choir, etc.?

What kinds of kids did you associate with?

Who were your best friends during high school?

Are you still in contact with them?

Did you work while attending school?

What did you do?

How much were you paid?

Who was the first boy/girl you ever kissed?

How old were you?

What were the circumstances?

Was it that first special kiss for you?

Did you have a crush on someone, but did not let them know?

Do you still feel that way?

If you could meet them today, would you say something to them?

What attracted you to them?

Who was the first person you were serious about?

Why did you feel that way?

Did you attend the senior prom?

Who was your date?

Where was it located?

What was it like?

If you could have changed one thing about high school years, what would it have been?

Learning to drive was a rite of passage. When did you learn to drive?

Have you ever had any accidents or tickets? Explain.

What was going on in your family when you were in high school?

What did you do when you were a teenager that got you in the most trouble, and how did your family handle it?

Do you remember any fads from your youth?

Popular hairstyles?

Clothes?

Can you remember any catchy words or phrases from your youth, i.e., groovy, dig it?

Outlook

Whom did you admire the most in your family when you were young?

Why?

Was there anyone outside your family whom you admired- neighbors, teachers, etc.?

Why?

When you were young, what did you hope to do when you grew up?

Did that pan out?

Were you happy as a child?

Did anything frighten you when you were young?

How did you learn to cope with it?

Where did you get your ideas and values?

Do you have a personality like that of someone else in your family? Is there anyone today whom you wish you could be more like from your childhood?

How would you sum up your childhood and adolescence?

Entertainment

When you were young, what type of music did you listen to?

What type of music did your parents like?

How was music brought into your home?

Did you play an instrument?

How did you learn to play it (them)?

What experience did you have in learning to play?

Practice. Was it a chore, or did you enjoy it?

Did you have a music teacher, or were you self-taught?

During the 50s and 60s, many parents were not happy with the music their kids were listening to. How did your parents view the music you listened to as a teenager?

Who were your favorite artists?

What influence did music have on you?

Did your family have a radio?

How old were you when they got one?

Did you listen to radio programs, i.e., Fibber McGee and Molly, Family Theater, The Fred Allen Show, etc.?

What was it like?

What were your favorite radio programs?

Had movies been invented when you were young?

If not, how old were you?

Were they silent or talkies?

What experience did you have?

What did the theater look like?

How much were the tickets back then?

Who was your favorite screen star?

What made them stand out to you?

What influence did movies have on you?

Did you go to the theater to see a play, opera, or symphony?

Do you remember what you saw and why did that or those stand out?

Did you ever see or meet any famous people from music, actors, or authors?

When did your family get their first TV?

What did it look like?

Was it a black and white or color TV?

How many channels did it have?

Did you have to get up to go change the channel?

What were some of the earliest programs that you watched?

Name some of your favorite programs you enjoyed over the years.

Did you enjoy reading?

What genre did you enjoy?

Has that changed over the years?

Who was your favorite author?

We have talked about sports. Would you prefer watching them on TV or going to the game?

Other Information

Did any natural disasters happen during your childhood?

How did your family cope with the situation?

Now that we have had to deal with Covid, were there any other epidemics that swept the nation, i.e., Spanish Flu, Hong Kong Flu, etc. and did any affect you or your family?

Were you a victim of measles, mumps, or other childhood illnesses?

Broken bones?

Hearing loss?

Did you ever have to go to the emergency room for treatment as a child?

Were you ever admitted to the hospital as a child?

What was the reason?

How did you feel about staying there?

Higher Education

What education did you acquire past high school?

Did you attend college?

Trade school?

If yes, when, and where did you attend school?

Why did you choose that field?

Why did you choose to attend that school?

Did you graduate?

How did you pay for your education?

Do you remember the cost for your education?

Did your family support, oppose, or encourage your education?

Who influenced you the most and helped you to develop your skills?

Think back to an incident during this time… what was going on?

In your eyes at the time, how was the world evolving?

Who were your friends from this period?

Are you still in contact with them?

Who did you date during this period of your life?

What sort of things did you do on your dates?

Is there anything that stands out as the most fun?

Did you work during this time in your life?

What did you do?

How much did you make?

If you could change the path you went on in college/trade school, what would it have been?

Leaving Home

When did you eventually leave the family home?

What were the circumstances?

Where did you go?

What did you do between the time you left home or graduated, and the time you got married?

What was your first job after you left home?

What other jobs did you have over the years?

Which one was the most challenging?

Which one did you enjoy the most and why?

Did you serve in the Armed Forces?

What made you decide to join the military?

What service did you join and when?

What were the major events in your military career?

Were you stationed overseas? Explain.

What was your highest rank when you were discharged?

What was your fondest memory serving?

What was your least favorite memory?

Marriage and Married Life

Did you ever marry or come close with someone other than my father/mother?

What is your spouse's name?

When, where, and how did you meet?

What did you do on your first date?

What was the courtship like?

When did you meet your future in-laws after you started dating?

How did the meeting go?

How long after you met your future spouse did you get married?

Describe the wedding, i.e., the venue, color theme, flowers, wedding dress, bridesmaid's dresses, men's clothing-tuxedo or casual, etc.

Where was the location?

Church?

Justice of the Peace?

Courthouse?

Destination wedding?

Was it a religious ceremony?

How long was the ceremony?

How large was the wedding?

How many were in the wedding party?

Who was the best man and maid of honor?

Who were the bridesmaids and groomsmen?

Did you have a flower girl and ring bearer?

Describe the reception.

Was it a formal, sit-down dinner?

Was it casual, finger foods type?

Describe the wedding and groom's cakes.

What type of music did they play?

Did you go on a honeymoon?

Where and how long did you stay?

If you could have changed anything about the wedding, reception, or honeymoon, what would that have been?

Where was your first home?

Describe the home, and the neighborhood.

Did you enjoy working in the garden and mowing the lawn?

How did you feel about house work?

How did you divide household responsibilities?

Since first marrying, how many houses did you live in?

What were the reasons for moving?

Which location was your favorite?

How did you and your spouse handle conflicts or disagreements?

What were some shared hobbies or activities you enjoy together?

Describe a memorable moment you have shared with your spouse.

How did you support each other's personal goals and aspirations?

Have you experienced any significant challenges in your marriage?

How did you overcome them?

How did you keep a bond in your relationship?

What traditions or rituals did you have as a couple?

How has your relationship evolved over time?

What advice would you give to newlyweds or couples navigating challenges in their marriage?

How did you celebrate milestones or anniversaries together?

Reflecting on your marriage, what are you most grateful for?

Did your spouse work outside the home?

Did you give parties in your home? Explain.

How long did the marriage last?

Why do you think the marriage lasted as long as it did?

If it ended in divorce, how did this marriage end?

How did your family feel about it ending?

Did you ever start over with another marriage?

For the second marriage, how did your family react to you remarrying?

How was this one different from the first marriage?

What do you say is the most important thing about choosing a spouse?

In what ways has marriage turned out to be different than you expected?

Family

Do you have any children?

If not, why didn't you have them?

How many children did you have?

What were their names, and where were they born?

What was their weight and length?

Think back to the day that your first child was born…what was the experience like for you?

How about the other children?

What was that experience like?

How did the other births differ from the first one?

What were their personalities, talents, or traits that make them different and special?

How did you raise them?

What were your discipline tactics?

What were some special memories of raising your children?

What is the best thing about children?

What was the most challenging for you?

Did they join any organizations such as scouts or sports?

Did you coach any of their teams, or become a den mother/father?

Did you join the PTA/PTO at their schools?

Did your family have any special traditions?

Christmas/Hanukkah/Easter/Fourth of July/Labor Day/Thanksgiving

How did you spend your birthdays with your family?

Are there any birthdays that stand out?

Did your family ever go on any vacations?

How often?

Where did you go?

Did any vacation stand out as being special for you?

Did your family have any pets?

What were they, and what were their names?

How long did they live?

Who was responsible for taking care of them?

What jobs did you hold during your lifetime?

What were some of your favorite books/authors you read, and would recommend?

Why?

What were your favorite magazines?

Why?

What were your favorite meals that you or your spouse cooked?

Who was the better cook in your house?

Where was the typical location where your family had their meals?

Did you eat out a lot?

What were your favorites restaurants?

Are they still in business?

Did you go to the movies, concerts, opera, or symphonies?

How often did you go?

Which did you like best?

Why?

What kind of vehicles did you and your family own?

Which was your favorite?

Why?

Which one did you not like?

Why?

Any stories about a particular car/truck?

Any accidents? Explain.

Did you own any recreational vehicles or boats?

Did you enjoy them?

What did you not like about them?

Did you have any interesting or important visitors to your house?

What was the reason, and how did the occasion go?

Did your family attend any family reunions?

Did you have any contact with any of your family members?

Which family members outside your immediate family do you miss seeing? Explain.

Were there any tragedies in your family that you would want to share?

Can you provide details about the event?

Later Years and Retirement

Are you still married?

Explain. Death, divorce? Give details.

How old were you when you retired?

Do you miss working?

If you could, would you go back to work?

Where do you live now?

Describe where you live, i.e., type of dwelling, location, neighborhood.

What is it like to be a grandparent?

Do you see them as often as you would like?

When you do, do you spoil them?

What is their favorite thing to do with you?

What is your favorite thing to do with them?

Do you enjoy traveling?

Where have you gone?

Would you return to any of the places you have been before?

What would you say has been your greatest adventure so far?

What interests or hobbies do you have?

Who is your best friend?

What do you have in common?

What do you like to do for fun?

Do you belong to any organizations?

What are your food preferences?

Do you enjoy eating out or staying at home and cooking?

What does the mail mean to you? Are you a good letter writer?

Do you correspond with anyone today?

Do you send out Christmas cards?

Do you have or use a computer?

Do you have and use a cell phone?

What has been the most difficult for you in terms of computers or cell phones?

Are you a gamer?

Are you on any social media?

Do you enjoy going shopping outside your home?

Does shopping frustrate you today since online shopping seems to be the better choice?

What is the most adventuresome thing you have ever done?

Do you think you could do it again?

What is the most wonderful thing that ever happened to you?

Now that you are at this stage of your life, what would you say to that little girl/boy that you were, about life?

History and You

From racial, political, and labor issues to wars, everyone has a cause. Did you ever join a protest or demonstration?

Black or white, male or female, young or old. Did anyone ever discriminate against you?

What was the situation, and can you elaborate?

What countries and events have held your interest over the years?

In the late 19th century, the US economic structure changed. Farmers and small businesses gave up their reign, and big business was born. How did this change affect your lifestyle?

When oil was discovered in Texas in 1901, did you or your family rush off to strike it rich?

What can you remember about the Titanic? Did it affect you in any way?

In WWI, President Woodrow Wilson had first declared the neutrality of the US, but we eventually became involved. At that time, did you think that was the right thing to do?

What did you think of his presidency?

From time spent overseas to time at home, WWI significantly affected many people's lives. How was your family involved in WWI?

The 1925 Scopes Trial was a landmark case, pitting "evolutionists" against "creationists." What side of the issue were you on?

Between 1920 and 1933, Prohibition was in effect. What were you doing during the Prohibition Era?

Were you a strict prohibitionist or a free-thinking flapper?

Did you ever go to Speak Easy?

How did the 1929 Stock Market Crash and ensuing Depression affect you and your family?

How did this experience influence your values?

Herbert Hoover was president then. How did you feel about his presidency?

Did you think Franklin D. Roosevelt's New Deal was the answer to the Depression?

Did the "alphabet soup" of programs that he created affect you? From 1939 to 1945, whether you were on the front lines or held down the home front, how did World War II affect you?

Do you feel we should have gone to Europe to fight the evilness of Hitler and Mussolini?

The Holocaust stands as one of the darkest chapters in human history. Can you expand on this?

Tell me about your experience with the bombing of Pearl Harbor.

Did you have any family who were involved with the conflict?

Roosevelt died during the war. How did you feel about Harry S. Truman becoming president?

Did you think he was going to be an effective leader?

Tell me about your experience with D-Day.

When and where were you when you found out that the war was over?

How did you celebrate?

What do you think would have happened here in America, if we had stayed out of the war?

How did your life change after WWII?

What did the Cold War stand for to you?

Did you fear that war would break out between the East and the West?

Did it seem too distant to worry about?

Did your family build a bomb shelter and stock food?

Did you have drills at school in case we were bombed?

In 1952, Dwight D. Eisenhower easily won the presidency because of his popularity in WWII.

What was life like for you during his administration?

Do you think he was an effective president?

What are your thoughts on the highway system that Eisenhower implemented?

How old were you, and what were you doing during the Korean War?

How did it influence your thoughts about US intervention overseas and Communism?

During the 1950s, the Red Scare was rampant in the US, causing everyone to be scared.

Were you caught up in it?

What was your opinion about Senator McCarthy?

Do you think he got what he deserved?

Brown v. Board of Education was a landmark case in its time, declaring that separate education was unequal and therefore unconstitutional.

Which side of the issue did you support and why?

Do you think it was effective?

What did you think about Kennedy sending "advisors" to Vietnam, and then troops started arriving over there?

Did you think this would last a long time?

How did you feel about the war?

Did you or any relatives go to Vietnam?

If you had a draft number, what was yours?

Did you lose any friends or family there?

What side did you take with the war?

How did you feel about the troops when they arrived back in the States?

Do you think we got all the POWs out of Vietnam?

May of 1961, Alan Shepard made his historic flight.

Were you fascinated by space exploration?

Did you stay home from school or work to watch it on TV?

In 1962, the Cuban Missile Crisis put the US on the brink of war with the Soviet Union. How old were you?

Did this prospect frighten you?

What did you think the outcome would be?

How did the schools help students prepare if there was a disaster?

What other thoughts do you have of this period?

Where were you, and what were you doing when you found out that John F. Kennedy had been assassinated?

How old were you?

Were you in school at the time?

What grade were you in?

Did they close your school after the event?

What was your reaction to the news?

Do you have an opinion about who killed him?

Between the Civil Rights Movement and Vietnam, what are your feelings about Lyndon B. Johnson as president?

Since 1923, women have been pushing for an Equal Rights Amendment.

In the 60s and 70s, the movement was strong. What are your feelings about the ERA?

Did you belong to the NOW (National Organization for Women)?

Do you think women have the same rights as men in this day and time?

Why do you feel that way?

Do you think things will change?

On July 20, 1969, the men of the Apollo 11 mission landed on the moon. How did you feel about the fact that the US was the first country to carry this out?

Do you think we will return to the moon?

Who was Martin Luther King Jr to you?

How did you feel about his ideas and methods?

What did you think of the marches and the violence at that time?

In 1969, Charles Manson and his followers murdered Sharon Tate and others in Los Angeles. To many, the randomness of his killings was frightening.

What did you think about Charles Manson and his followers?

How did this affect your emotions?

Do you think he should have gone back to the death penalty after the state reinstated it?

In 1972, Richard Nixon visited both China and the USSR. What did you think of his actions?

Did you feel that the US should deal with a Communist country?

What did you believe about Nixon's involvement in Watergate?

Were you glad that he resigned?

Do you think President Gerald Ford should have pardoned Nixon?

From gas lines to unemployment, people felt the oil crunch in many ways.

How were you affected by the OPEC Oil Embargo against the US?

Do you remember waiting in long lines to get ten gallons of gas every other day?

In all your years, what is the cheapest gas that you bought?

What did you think of the Iranian Hostage Crisis, and how was it handled?

Did terrorism make you afraid to travel?

Were you interested in the space shuttle voyages?

Did you watch the Challenger explosion?

In 1987, Gorbachev and Ronald Reagan signed a peace treaty limiting missiles.

Do you think it will last?

What did you think when Reagan told Gorbachev to "tear down this wall?"

What did you think of Reagan's presidency?

How old were you, and what were you doing when the Berlin Wall came down in 1989?

How did you feel about it?

Did you think it would happen in your lifetime?

What are your feelings about President George H. W. Bush and the Persian Gulf War?

Should we have killed Saddam Hussein at that time while we were there?

What do you think of Bill Clinton's presidency?

Do you think he was an honest president?

What do you think of Hillary Clinton? Do you think she is an honest person?

What do you think of George W. Bush's presidency?

Where were you on September 11, 2001, when you got the news that the World Trade Center was hit by the airplanes?

What were your first thoughts?

What did you do after hearing about it?

Did you have any relatives who were lost that day?

How did it affect you?

How long did it take you to process the information and get through it?

Was there anything you did, i.e., go to New York and help, send money, clothes, etc., for the people who were involved?

Do you think Bush handled the situation well?

Do you think that 9/11 shaped his presidency for the better or worse?

Do you think we should have gone to Iraq and removed Hussein?

What do you think of our involvement now in Iraq?

Will we always be there for peace keeping missions?

What are your thoughts on Barack Obama?

How do you feel about Obamacare healthcare?

Do you think it was a good reform?

How do you feel about America since the election of Donald Trump?

Do you feel he was an effective president?

How do you feel about him reshaping the federal judiciary?

When Covid hit, how did it affect you and your family?

How old were you?

Did anyone you know die from it?

Do you think Trump handled the situation properly?

How about emotionally?

Did you have to stop working or do everything online?

How did you feel about shopping and wearing masks everywhere?

Do you feel safe now?

President Joe Biden is the oldest president to date.

Do you think there should be an age limit on the presidency?

Do you think he has been an effective president?

Do you think the conflicts over the centuries with Israel will ever be resolved?

Do you think history's truths change over the years?

52

History is ongoing and since this book has been published, there are many more questions that could be asked. Please add those that you feel would be important for this interview.

Philosophy and Religion

What did you learn in your life that you would pass on to others?

How did your free time contribute to your personality?

Do you have a philosophy of life to share with your descendants?

Do you have a favorite philosopher, teacher, or writer who best expresses your philosophy?

What is your religious affiliation, or are you a spiritualist?

Have your religious leanings changed over the years?

If so, how?

Do you follow your parents' beliefs?

Do you have a favorite scripture?

What feelings or thoughts does it provoke?

Have you read the entire Bible?

How many times?

Do you have a favorite religious song?

Why that one?

If you are spiritual, have you contacted your spiritual guide?

How far have you gotten into your spirituality?

Have you ever had a near-death experience?

Can you explain it?

How did that change your life?

What is your experience with answers to prayers?

Has anybody in the family ever had any unusual psychic abilities or special powers such as life-after-death experiences, mediumship, clairvoyance, and other Claire abilities?

Have any of those powers been passed on in the family?

What are things you believe and know are true?

In your opinion, which have been the greatest advances or inventions of all?

What are your thoughts on electric cars that can drive themselves?

Do you have one, or do you think you will ever get one?

What things have given you the most pleasure or satisfaction?

In one word, how do you live successfully?

What do you consider to be your most important achievements?

Is there anything that has caused you perpetual concern?

What events or trends have disturbed you most in your lifetime?

Is there anything that frightens you today?

How do you feel about winning or losing?

What brings you the most peace and why?

What is the most trying experience you have ever had?

What lesson did you learn from it?

What is the biggest lesson in life you found to be true?

Everyone has a talent. What do you think yours is?

If you had known then what you know now, what would you have done differently in your life?

Have you ever stood up for what you believe, even when it was hard? Tell me about it.

What are your goals now?

What do you think will be the major events of the next ten years?

Did you think the past ten years have changed so dramatically?

Why do you feel that way?

For some advice for your great-grandchildren…what would you say to them about the area of education?

What about choosing and managing a career?

What advice would you give them about money?

What would you say about love and marriage?

What about how to raise a family?

Since future generations of your family will be reading/watching this, what do you have to say to them?

What do you hope your legacy will be?

Is there anything else you would like to add or say to complete this?

Final Thoughts

And there you have it! What an incredible achievement you have accomplished. Enhance it further by gathering photos, documents, and other memorabilia to give it a personal touch. When you are ready to convert it into a physical book, various printing companies offer options for binding, whether it be a hard or soft cover. Alternatively, your local print shop could assist you. Your family will undoubtedly cherish this historical account, gaining deeper insights into their life's journey. If you have any questions or comments, please email me at yourlivingyears24@gmail.com.